BLANCHE LESLIE;

OR THE

LIVING ROSARY.

p. 25.

LONDON:

JAMES BURNS, 17 PORTMAN STREET,
PORTMAN SQUARE.

BLANCHE LESLIE;

OR THE

LIVING ROSARY.

"HERE is Miss Leslie, here is Miss Leslie!" cried a number of young voices, as a wheel-chair drove slowly up to the play-green which fronted the pretty school-house in the village of Leslie. It was surrounded in a moment by all the village children, and innumerable were the exclamations and questions addressed to its occupant; among which, inquiries after her health were the most frequently and earnestly repeated.

Blanche Leslie was the only child and

heiress of a country gentleman of great
wealth and influence, who died before
she had attained the eighth year of her
age. She had lost her mother when
quite an infant, and since the death
of her father had always resided at
Leslie House under the care of her
guardian, who was, likewise, a distant
relation. It was whispered in the village that she was not so happy as she
might have been, and that she pined
for a mother's care and a mother's love,
to soften the sufferings of her solitary
childhood,—for she was born a cripple,
and was even now, at the age of fifteen, a
prey to a mortal disorder which threat-
ened, in a few months more, to bring
her to an early grave. No one, however,
had ever heard even a whisper of com-
plaint fall from her lips ; she was ever
the same, patient, gentle, and submis-
sive ; and though her features were
shrunk and wasted by disease, the se-
raph sweetness of her smile made her
at times seem beautiful in the eyes of
all who loved her. And who did not
love Blanche Leslie ? Every one pitied
her sufferings, and admired her for the
patience with which they were endured.
But of her many friends, the village

people and the village children were ever the dearest of all to her. Regularly as the village clock struck four, her invalid chair drove up to the playground of the school-house, and she spent the next two hours in the midst of the young village girls, entering into all their joys and sorrows as if she had been one of them herself, and endeavouring to promote their true welfare by making religion seem lovely in their eyes.

It was the eve of the Assumption of the Blessed Virgin, and she had obtained a half-holiday for them, that they might assist her in adorning the village church for the festival. This was always the greatest pleasure she could give them; and soon after her arrival, a shout of delight hailed the arrival of a cart filled with evergreens and large baskets of flowers. Miss Leslie easily disposed of the boys by sending them with the gardener to adorn the church with the evergreens, and she then made the girls sit down on the grass around her chair to assist her in wreathing the flowers into garlands.

"How fond you are of roses, Miss Leslie!" said a little girl, as she handed her a basket of the beautiful flowers;

" I think you love them the best of all."

" I love all flowers," said Blanche, gently; " for they all are beautiful, and have all holy and happy thoughts for me."

" But what sort of thoughts have they got for you, Miss Leslie?" asked little Rose, who was the youngest of the party, and a great favourite with her young mistress.

" The wallflower, which blossoms so brightly upon old ruined walls, reminds me of the love and gratitude we should feel towards those who have taken care of our childhood, and how we should make their old age beautiful by our tenderness and care. The orange and the myrtle, which are so sweet when you crush their leaves, tell me of the usefulness of suffering, when it draws forth the sweet odour of patience from the sorrowing soul. The silvery bells of the lily of the valley, hiding themselves among their long green leaves, speak to me of the modesty with which all young girls should endeavour to withdraw themselves from the praise and notice of others. And I never see the violet, so humble and yet so sweet, without thinking of the virtuous poor, whose good and holy lives are as full of fragrance to our heavenly Father as the odour of the violet is to us."

"But the rose—the rose; you have said nothing of your favourite rose, Miss Leslie," cried several of her listeners.

"The rose," answered Blanche, bending her head with a look of reverence as she spoke, "ever reminds me of the holy inhabitants of the stable of Bethlehem—of Jesus, Mary, and Joseph. The red rose tells me of the infinite charity of Jesus, who poured forth His blood like water upon the earth for the salvation of mankind. The white rose, of the purity of Joseph, who was deemed worthy to be the guardian of the Virgin Mother of God; and the moss-rose, which wraps a covering of moss round its delicate buds, of the maternal affection of Mary, who strove to preserve her shivering infant from the cold in the shelter of her bosom. But I think oftenest of Jesus when I see the rose, because Scripture calls Him the lily of the valley and the rose of Sharon; and because on the fourth Sunday of Lent the Pope blesses and embalms a golden rose adorned with jewels, pronouncing over it some beautiful prayers, in which Jesus is styled, 'The eternal Rose that has gladdened and embalmed the world.'"

"Do tell us something more about the rose, while we go on working, Miss Leslie."

"I will tell you two pretty stories which I read the other day; the first is about the dear St. Elizabeth, as the old writers love to call her. She was very charitable, and spent all that she possessed in relieving the poor. One day she was leaving the castle in which she lived, with her apron full of provisions for them, when she met her husband, who was curious to know what it was she carried with so much care. Though Elizabeth was a royal princess, she was not ashamed of the menial nature of her employment, but she did not wish her husband to know it, lest her charity should attract his admiration. After a little struggle, however, he succeeded in making her drop the apron, when, instead of the provisions he expected to behold, a quantity of beautiful roses fell to the ground. It was in the middle of winter, so there could be no doubt of the miracle, and all who beheld it were filled with astonishment at the manner in which God rewarded the humility of this charitable princess."

"What a pretty story!" said little Rose; "pray, Miss Leslie, tell us another."

"Only one more, then," said Miss Leslie, and she instantly began. "Once upon a time a hermit built himself a cell very near the banks of a swift-flowing river. He lived here for many years, and his reputation for sanctity brought many people to visit him, so that at last he began to entertain thoughts of pride, which were very displeasing to Almighty God. One morning he was about to cross the river to visit a distant church, when he beheld a man sitting on the bank, and weeping most bitterly. The hermit instantly recognised him as a notorious robber who had filled the whole country with terror by his crimes. Very much astonished, he was about to proceed on his way, when the man flung himself at his feet, declaring his sins, and entreating to know if he might ever hope for their pardon. Now while the hermit listened to this recital of terrible crime, he thought with complacency on his own blameless life, and, filled with pride and indignation, he exclaimed: 'Dost thou hope for pardon, thou wicked sinner? Sooner shall roses bloom upon this dry staff in my hand, than a just God grant forgiveness to such sins as thine.' When the poor robber heard this harsh sentence, he sat down by the bank of the river weeping more bitterly than before, and the hermit haughtily pursued his way. He had not, however, gone very far when the staff which he carried in his hand stuck fast in the ground; he endeavoured to pull it out, but the harder he pulled, the faster it seemed to become rooted in the earth. Then, while he stood still with astonishment, he beheld bud and leaf and flower sprouting rapidly out, until at last the dry stick was laden with beautiful roses, and at the same time he heard a voice saying close to his ear: 'Sooner shall roses bloom on the barren stick, than a good God refuse mercy to the repenting sinner, or grant it to the proud one.' Filled with shame and contrition, the hermit fell on his knees and bewailed his fault with many tears; after which he rose up, and once more endeavoured to release his staff. This time it yielded easily to his grasp, and he then returned to the spot where he had left the robber, and shewing him the stick all covered with roses, he said : 'See, brother, the wonder which God hath wrought to shew forth His acceptance of your tears, and to convince me of my fault. Be of good cheer, therefore, and weep no more, but come with me to my cell, and together we will mourn over our sins for the rest of our days, so that we may claim His mercy in the days that are to come.'   Much comforted, the robber dried his tears, and followed the hermit to his cell.   They planted the staff before the door, and it soon grew up into a beautiful tree. Here they lived together for many years in holiness and brotherly love, and both dying on the same day in great sentiments of devotion, the rose tree shed forth a fragrance which was perceived by the country people many miles from the spot, and was considered by them as a sign of their eternal beatification ; and it passed into a sort of proverb among them, 'that God would sooner cause roses to bloom on the barren stick, than refuse mercy to the sinner who implored it at His hands.'   So you see," continued Miss Leslie, "that the rose is particularly the emblem of charity, and should therefore most of all remind us of the good Jesus, whose burning love induced Him to suffer and die for our salvation."

"How fast you work, Miss Leslie!" said one of the girls; "you have finished that wreath of red roses while you were telling us this pretty story."

"Yes, and now I must begin a white one for the image of our Blessed Lady. Tell me, all of you, would you not like to offer a crown of roses at her altar every day in the year?"

"Oh, very much!" cried little Rose. "But we could not do that, you know, Miss Leslie, for in our little garden roses flower only for a very short time in the summer."

"That is very true," said Blanche, "and even in a conservatory they could scarcely be forced in sufficient quantities. I did not mean that, little Rose. There is another way in which even the poorest among you can offer roses to Mary all the year round, if you like."

"Do pray tell us how! oh, do pray tell us how, Miss Leslie!" cried a number of eager voices.

Blanche opened the "Daily Com-

pauion," and made one of the elder
girls read aloud the prayer which fol-
lows the last glorious mystery of the
Rosary.

"You observe," she then continued,
"that we here beg of our Blessed Lady
to accept the rosary which, as a crown
of roses, we offer at her feet. By never
omitting to say the beads, we are then
really offering to her the kind of roses
she loves the best, that is to say, we are
giving her the tribute of our love, and
of our sympathy in all her earthly sorrows and all her heavenly consolations."

Some of the children looked rather
blank at hearing this, and Rose ven-
tured to say : "But the beads are so
very very long, Miss Leslie; and poor
little girls like we are can hardly find
time to say them, because when we are
not at school, we are almost always
wanted to work at home."

"You are quite right," answered
Blanche; "and the work which you do
well for your parents will be more ac-
ceptable to God than all the prayers
you could possibly say. But there is
another way of saying the rosary, which
is particularly suited to poor children
who have not much time to give to

prayer. There are fifteen mysteries in
the rosary, and supposing each of us
agreed to say one Our Father and ten
Hail Mary's during the course of the day
in honour of some particular mystery,
we should among us lay the crown of
roses, which is mentioned in the prayer
you have just read, at the feet of Mary."

"Oh, we should all like that very
much indeed," said one of her listeners.

"Well, then, I have written out the
mysteries on cards, and we can each
draw for one, which we will agree to
say during the course of the month;
at the end of that time the cards must
be changed, and we will draw for them
over again."

By Blanche's direction, fourteen of
the elder girls each drew a card accord-
ing to their age, the fifteenth she re-
served for herself. The mystery was
the "Assumption," and the virtue to be
practised was "union with God."

A smile of pleasure gave for one moment a seraphic beauty to her pallid
face as she read the words aloud.

"But how are we to practise all these
virtues, Miss Leslie? some of them
seem so very difficult."

"They seem so perhaps," said Miss

Leslie; "but if you give me your cards, I will try and make them more easy to understand. Humility is the virtue attached to the mystery of the Annunciation. If when you are reproved by your parents or superiors, you do not try to excuse yourself, but submit with patience to the reproof, even though it should chance to be undeserved—you will, I think, have practised as much of this virtue as can be expected from you. To the Visitation belongs the virtue of charity. It can easily be practised by little acts of kindness to your neighbours, or by yielding your own wishes to those of your young companions. Poverty is the virtue for the Nativity. You are poor already, but you will practise the virtue of poverty of spirit by trying always to be contented with the situation in which God has placed you, and by repressing all feelings of envy towards those who are better off than yourselves. If you were rich, I should tell you to endeavour not to love money, but to regard it as a gift which God has sent you rather to be employed in the relief of the poor, than for the gratification of your own selfish wishes. Obedience is for the Presenta-

tion.   In obedience to the will of God
Mary offered her little Jesus in the Tem-
ple.   You must try and practise this
virtue by ready compliance with the
wishes of your parents, who represent
Him in your regard.   Tell me, do you
understand all this?"

"Oh, certainly," said an elder girl;
"but how can I practise my virtue—
desire of being united to God? that is
so difficult."

Something in Blanche's face seemed
to say it was not very difficult to her;
but she only answered :

"Perhaps it is so to young and happy
children.   But think sometimes for a
minute how much happier the Saints
are in the society of God, and say a
short prayer to Him that He Himself
may confer upon you the grace of desire
to behold Him in His glory.

"The next card is 'the Agony' and
the virtue of resignation.'   If any thing
happen contrary to your wishes; if the
day is wet when you wish it to be fine;
if you are compelled to work at home
when you would prefer going out to play
in the fields, then make an offering of
your own will to Almighty God, and you
will have practised something of the

virtue which Jesus gave to your imitation, when He cried out in the garden, 'Father, Thy will, not mine, be done.'

"The 'Scourging at the pillar' comes next, and the virtue is 'penance.' Sometimes deny yourself a little pleasure, the smelling of a fragrant flower, the leaving one little morsel on your plate at dinner. This, I should think, will be mortification enough for such young girls as you are."

"But these are such very little things, Miss Leslie."

"It is only by frequent self-denial in little things that we can ever hope to deny ourselves in great ones," answered Miss Leslie. "The 'Crowning with thorns,' and 'Love of humiliation,' is the next card. And to practise this virtue, you must try to be contented, if you cannot be joyful, when you see any one preferred to yourself. If, for instance, one of your schoolfellows get a higher place in the class than you have, try and overcome your own momentary feeling of discontent, and afterwards say something kind to her on the occasion. By accepting the little humiliation in this manner, you will gain far greater merit than you are aware of. The same may be said of the 'Good use of sufferings' which is the virtue for the 'Carrying the cross.' A little sickness, or other annoyance, borne cheerfully, is more pleasing in the sight of God than any voluntary penance you could impose on yourselves. If you have had any little quarrel with your companions, and readily forgive them, you will have complied with the precept of pardoning your enemies, which is the virtue for the mystery of the Crucifixion."

" But our companions are not really our enemies," said one of the girls.

" I hope you will never have any real enemies," Blanche answered. " It will, therefore, be sufficient if you forgive the momentary annoyance your friends may cause you. Lively faith is the virtue of the 'Resurrection.' Ask sometimes for the virtue of faith, and say in your heart, 'O my God, I believe in Thee! do Thou increase my faith.' When you frequently fall into the same fault, and almost despair of overcoming yourself, say in your heart, 'Though I can do nothing of myself, Almighty God can do all things in me. I will therefore still hope that He will, at last, give me grace to conquer this failing.' This is the virtue of hope, as it is to be practised for the mystery of the Ascension."

"I have got the 'Descent of the Holy Ghost,' and 'Zeal for saving souls.' But how can I practise that virtue? I cannot go and preach to people, can I, Miss Leslie?"

"You would do very little good if you did," said Blanche, smiling. "You need not preach to sinners; but you must pray for them, and give them good example. More souls are saved in this way, than by long sermons. The 'Crowning of the Blessed Virgin,' is the last and fifteenth card. When you say the 'Hail Mary' in your morning prayers, try and say it with the loving confidence a little child feels when it speaks to its mother, and this will be the best way in which to practise the virtue of 'Confidence in Mary' attached to the mystery."

"But you have said nothing of your own mystery, the 'Assumption.'"

"The virtue for the Assumption is, 'Union with God.' To practise this virtue, I must endeavour to keep my will perfectly united with the holy will of God ; neither wishing nor asking for any thing but that which He is pleased to send me; whether it be joy, or sorrow, health or sickness, or even death itself. And now, I must warn you, that in all probability, you will not find it easy to practise most of these virtues at first; I would, therefore, advise you in the beginning, to make a resolution to do so two or three times during the month for the intention of the rosary, and thus in time, I think, they will become easy and habitual to you. Of course you are bound to be always charitable to your neighbours, and obedient to your superiors; but you might manage sometimes to do an act of unsolicited kindness to your companions, or to give a more prompt obedience to your parents; and in time, such acts will grow into a habit with you ; and you will do them almost without being conscious of it. Will you tell me," added Blanche, anxiously, " if I have made all this clear to you ?"

" I think I understand what you mean, Miss Leslie; and will you tell us please when we are to begin?" said one of the children.

" The first Sunday in October is the

Feast of the Rosary. I think we had better wait and begin on that day : we will all ask leave to go to holy communion in the morning, to gain the indulgence granted to the members of the Society of the Rosary ; and in the afternoon I invite you all to come and dine with me at Leslie House ; and I hope we shall spend a very happy evening together. Rose, my child, what is the matter with you ?" said Blanche, turning suddenly round ; for her quick ear caught the sounds of the little girl's sobs, as she stood behind the others, vainly endeavouring to check her tears.

" It is because there are fourteen girls without me ; and so I am not in the Rosary."

Miss Leslie glanced her eye over the group. It was very true ; the holders of the cards were all older, and had therefore a better claim than poor Rose to a place in the Rosary ; and the other children were far too young to make it proper to join them in a devotion which requires regular and daily prayer from all its members.

" Never mind," said Blanche, kindly ; " have a little patience, Rose ; and I promise you that in a very few

months you will have a card in our Rosary."

" But how can that be?" asked the
sobbing Rose; " for in a few months
they will all be just as much older than
me as they are to-day."

" It is very true; they will, Rose.
But, still, I think it will be as I say.
And you may rely on my word; for
you know that I would not willingly
deceive you."

Blanche's word was always law to
all her village-children, and Rose never
thought of doubting her now, so she
returned, contented and happy, to her
employment.

The first Sunday in October was a
happy day for the young girls of the
" Living Rosary." On the preceding
evening Blanche had brought each of
them a white dress for the occasion;
and she made the same present to her
favourite little Rose, with an assurance
that she would soon want it as a mem-
ber of their society. They received
the holy communion in the morning,
and said the rosary directly after Mass,
but it was agreed that, in future, they
should meet in the church at four
o'clock; and that each of them should

then recite to herself her own particular share of it. Miss Leslie thought this the best way of ensuring its regular performance among her young associates. Blanche dined with them in a tent placed upon the lawn, and did her best to seem well and cheerful, but she was suffering sadly, and before the conclusion of dinner fainted from over-fatigue, and was carried to her chamber. It was evident to all around her, that her disorder had reached its crisis, and that she was rapidly sinking; but Blanche would not allow her dear children to be made sorrowful by the knowledge of her danger; and it was not until nightfall that they received a summons to the chamber of their young mistress, and were told that she had already received all the last consolations of our holy religion. Checking their tears and sobs as well as they could, they knelt quietly around her bed; for they understood that it was her wish to say the rosary once more among them before she died. Blanche made a sign to Rose to kneel close to her pillow; and she placed her own rosary card in the little girl's hand, "You will say it for me to-night, and this month, dear Rose"—she whispered, faintly, "next month it will be your own, as I told you."—

"But I did not want it in this way," sobbed Rose. "Not by your death, Miss Leslie."

Blanche clasped her hands devoutly together, and whispered softly, "The will of God, Rose, the will of God! In life or in death, the holy and adorable will of God!"

She was thinking of the virtue on her card—"Union with God." And she looked so like an angel at this moment, that Rose wept no longer, as she gazed upon her. Then each of the girls (beginning at the Annunciation) said aloud her own mystery as well as her tears would let her; and when it was Rose's turn to recite the decade for the Assumption, Blanche turned her face towards the place where she knelt, and put her hand on the card, as if to express her entire acquiescence in the Divine pleasure which consigned her to an early grave. Rose finished her task with some difficulty, for tears almost choked her utterance; the girl next to her said the last mystery, "the Crowning of the Blessed Virgin," and read the little prayer which concludes the devotion; directly afterwards, Blanche half raised herself in bed,—smiled upon them as if to thank them for their kindness,—took the card from Rose, pressed it to her bosom, and instantly expired; bearing with her the prayers of her young companions, as a crown of precious roses, to lay at Mary's feet, when she claimed her intercession at the throne of her Son.

Blanche Leslie had made it her dying request that her funeral should be conducted as similar ceremonies are performed in Catholic countries for the members of the Society of the Rosary. Her coffin, therefore, with its white pall, which spoke truly of the youth and innocence of her it covered, was placed in the church, and her young companions of the " Living Rosary," dressed in white, and bearing lighted tapers in their hands, knelt around it while the Solemn Mass was being said for the repose of her soul.

Two and two, they afterwards followed the coffin to the solitary nook in the churchyard which Blanche had herself chosen for her last repose; and when the grave was filled up, and the mourners had all departed, the young girls lingered still, while they said the rosary aloud once more as a last tribute of gratitude to her who had established this holy devotion among them.

Some years afterwards I visited the spot. The grave of Blanche was covered with moss, and had been kept perfectly free of weeds, and three rose-trees had been planted round it—a red, a white, and a moss rose, in memory of her love for these beautiful flowers. The clergyman of the village told me they had been placed there by the Rosary girls, who still cherished her memory, and watched over her grave with affectionate gratitude. I asked after Rose; she had entered a convent. Of the others, some were happily married; others were settled in excellent situations; but he assured me that the pious practice which Blanche Leslie had established just before her death was still kept up by the children of the village; and he attributed much of the peace and happiness which reigned among them to the powerful protection of the Queen of Heaven, granted to them in consideration of the undiminished fervour with which they still persevered in the daily devotion of the "Living Rosary."

LONDON:
PRINTED BY LEVEY, ROBSON, AND FRANKLYN,
Great New Street, Fetter Lane.